Puccini

for Piano Solo

T0055366

ISBN 978-0-634-04098-6

RICORDI

DISTRIBUTED BY

HAL•LEONARD®

CONTENTS

LA BOHÈME [lah boh-**ehm**] (The Bohemian Life)
Opera in 4 acts
Libretto by Giuseppe Giacosa and Luigi Illica, after Henry Murger's novel *Scènes de la Vie de Bohème*
First performance: Teatro Regio, Turin; February 1, 1896

The story of this opera, one of the best loved in the repertory, is set in 1830s Paris, though productions of the opera are often set in the 1890s, the period of the opera's composition. Four friends share a garret apartment: the poet Rodolfo, the painter Marcello, the musician Schaunard, and the philosopher Colline. On a cold Christmas Eve, Rodolfo sends his roommates out to the Cafè Momus while he tries to finish a newspaper article. His neighbor Mimi, a seamstress, knocks on the door and asks him to light her candle. The two are immediately attracted to each other, and when Mimi "accidentally" drops her key and Rodolfo's candle "accidentally" goes out, they look for her key in the dark. In the aria "Che gelida manina" [kay **jeh**-lee-dah mah-**nee**-nah] (How cold your little hand is) he tells Mimi about himself and his life. She returns the favor in "Mi chiamano Mimì" [mee k'**yah**-mah-noh mee-**mee**] (I'm called Mimi), and by the end of the first act they are singing the love duet "O soave fanciulla" [oh soh-**ah**-vay fahn-**choo**-lah] (O gentle maiden). In act two they join the others at the Momus. Musetta, a coquettish cafè singer and Marcello's former lover, arrives, drawing attention to herself by singing the waltz-song "Quando men vo" [**kwan**-doh mehn voh] (When I go out). In her act three aria "Donde lieta" [**dohn**-day lee-**eh**-tah] (From the place she left), Mimi bids Rodolfo "farewell, without rancor." They quarrel, then say goodbye in the duet "Addio sogno d'amor" [ahd-**dee**-oh **sohn**-yoh dah-**mohr**] (Farewell, dream of love), just as Marcello and Musetta are reconciled. As the final act opens, Rodolfo and Marcello, too lovesick to work, sing the duet "O Mimì, tu piu non torni" [oh mee-**mee** too p'yoo nohn **tohr**-nee] (O Mimì, you do not return). Word arrives that Mimi is dying of tuberculosis; she soon comes back to the garret to be with Rodolfo. Colline decides to sell his beloved overcoat to get money for medicine, singing "Vecchia zimarra" [**vek**-ee-ah zee-**mahr**-rah] (Shabby old overcoat), and when the two lovers are left alone, Mimi sings "Sono andati" [**soh**-noh ah-**dah**-tee] (Are they gone). Mimi and Rodolfo renew their love for each other and share reminiscences. With all their bohemian friends present, Mimi dies peacefully, with Rodolfo sobbing over her lifeless body.

LA FANCIULLA DEL WEST [lah fahn-**choo**-lah dehl wehst] (The Girl of the Golden West)
Opera in 3 acts
Libretto by Carlo Zangarini and Guelfo Civinini, after David Belasco's play
First performance: Metropolitan Opera, New York; December 10, 1910

This opera, commissioned by the Metropolitan Opera, is set in a California mining camp during the 1849 gold rush. Minnie, proprietor of the Polka saloon, is adored and respected by the miners. Sheriff Jack Rance sings of his passion for her in the aria "Minnie, dalla mia casa son partito" [**min**-nee dahl-lah **mee**-ah **kah**-sah sohn pahr-**tee**-toh] (Minnie, I left my home). Minnie falls in love with Dick Johnson, a newcomer. Johnson is really the hunted bandit Ramerrez, but he tells her he wants to change his ways because of his love for her. After he is shot by a posse, she protects Johnson by hiding him in her house, but Sheriff Rance finds him there. Minnie challenges the sheriff to a poker game over Johnson, which she wins by cheating. Johnson is allowed to escape briefly, but is soon caught and sentenced to die by hanging. With a noose around his neck, he sings the aria "Ch'ella mi creda" [**kehl**-lah mee **kray**-dah] (Let her believe), in which he asks the miners to let Minnie believe he has escaped. Minnie rides in and begs the miners, who dote on her, to allow the two of them to leave together. The miners agree, and Minnie and Dick ride off into the sunset, singing "Addio, California."

GIANNI SCHICCHI [**jahn**-nee **skee**-kee]
Opera in 1 act
Libretto by Giovacchino Forzano, suggested by an episode in Dante's *Inferno*
First performance: Metropolitan Opera, New York; December 14, 1918

This comic opera, the third part of *Il trittico* (The Triptych), relates the story of the crime for which Gianni Schicchi, a real-life character, is consigned to hell in Dante's *Divine Comedy*. The action is set in Florence, 1299. The recently-deceased Buoso Donati is surrounded by falsely grieving relatives who become outraged when they learn that his will leaves his entire estate to a monastery. Rinuccio, one of Donati's young nephews, is in love with Lauretta, but his family disapproves of this union because they believe she is not worthy of the family. It is Rinuccio who finds the will, but he refuses to hand it over until the family promises they will engage the cunning Gianni Schicchi, Lauretta's father, to help them out of their dilemma, and also consent to his wedding plans. In his aria "Firenze è come un albero fiorito" [fih-**rent**-say ay **koh**-may oon **ahl**-beh-roh f'yoh-**ree**-toh] (Florence is like a flowering tree), Rinuccio extols Florence's past glories and acclaims Gianni Schicchi as yet another in the city's rich heritage of noble citizens. When Schicchi arrives he is loath to assist the money-hungry relatives. Lauretta, in love with Rinuccio, pleads with him in the famous aria "O mio babbino caro" [oh **mee**-oh bahb-**bee**-noh **kah**-roh] (O my beloved daddy). He agrees to help, orders the dead man removed, and warns the relatives of the punishment all will face if the plot is discovered (exile and the loss of a hand). He climbs into bed and dictates a new will to a gullible lawyer, leaving the choice items to himself and the house to Lauretta and Rinuccio.

MADAMA BUTTERFLY
Opera in 3 acts
Libretto by Giuseppe Giacosa and Luigi Illica, after the play by David Belasco, based on a story by John Luther Long
First performance: La Scala, Milan; February 17, 1904

The opera takes place in Nagasaki, Japan in the early 1900s. Lieutenant B.F. Pinkerton is an American naval officer stationed in Japan. In the aria "Amore o grillo" [**ah**-moh-ray oh **gree**-loh] (Love or whim), he tells the American consul Sharpless about his bride-to-be. Cio-Cio San, a 15-year-old geisha known as Madame Butterfly, has agreed to a broker-arranged marriage with him, giving up her religion for his and suffering the reproof of her family on her wedding day. Dressed in a Japanese wedding gown and surrounded by many female attendants, she makes one of the most melodically beautiful entrances in all of opera ("Entrance of Butterfly"). Pinkerton is less serious about the union, toasting the day he will have a "real American wife." When he soon leaves for America, he promises to come back "when the robin nests." Cio-Cio San waits for him, now with his son whom she has borne. After three years with no word from him, Butterfly still believes he will return, singing "Un bel dì vedremo" [oon behl dee veh-**dray**-moh] (One fine day he will return). Despite a marriage proposal from a rich Japanese suitor and efforts from Sharpless to make the true situation known to her, Butterfly believes that if Pinkerton hears of his Japanese son, he will return to her ("Che tua madre" [kay **too**-ah **mah**-dray]). Pinkerton's ship finally returns. Butterfly and her maid Suzuki adorn the house with cherry blossoms ("Flower Duet"), and keep vigil on the night before his coming. Upon arriving at Butterfly's home while she is out, he realizes the cruelty of his actions and sings a heartfelt goodbye to the house in the aria "Addio fiorito asil" [ahd-**dee**-oh f'yoh-**ree**-toh ah-**seel**] (Farewell, happy home). After he has left, Cio-Cio San rushes in expecting to find him there, but is faced with the truth in the person of the American wife, Kate Pinkerton. She will give up her son, she says, if Pinkerton will come for him in half an hour. Unwilling to live life with such shame, Butterfly says goodbye to her child, stabs herself with her father's sword, and dies just as Pinkerton enters to claim the boy.

MANON LESCAUT [mah-nõ leh-**sko**]
Opera in 4 acts
Libretto by Marco Praga, Domenico Oliva, Giuseppe Giacosa, Luigi Illica, after Abbè Prèvost's novel
   L'Histoire du Chevalier des Grieux et de Manon Lescaut
First performance: Teatro Regio, Turin; February 1, 1893

The opera is set in France and Louisiana in the late eighteenth century. The aria "Donna non vidi mai" [**dohn**-nah nohn **vee**-dee mah-ee] (I never saw such a beautiful woman) is sung by the Chevalier des Grieux when he sees Manon for the first time. She is on her way to a convent, under the care of her brother. Des Grieux speaks to her, they fall immediately in love and run off to Paris, stealing a carriage in which wealthy old Geronte di Ravoir, the Treasurer General, had himself hoped to abduct the girl. Eventually Manon leaves des Grieux, unable to resist Geronte's money. Wishing she could be back in the humble setting where she was truly loved, she complains that in the silken curtains ("In quelle trine morbide" [een **kwel**-leh **tree**-neh **mohr**-bee-day]) there is a chill that numbs her. When the Chevalier later reappears, the two pledge renewed love. Before fleeing together, Manon stops to gather up the jewels Geronte had lavished upon her. The delay is costly, for the police Geronte had summoned now enter and capture her. Manon is deported to Louisiana, and des Grieux insists on accompanying her. The orchestral Intermezzo is played between the scene of her banishment and the scene in America. In New Orleans, des Grieux helps Manon escape and they leave in search of an English settlement. At one point she finds herself ill, exhausted, and alone in the wilderness; she sings the dramatic aria "Sola, perduta, abbandonata" [**soh**-lah pehr-**doo**-tah ahb-bahn-doh-**nah**-tah] (Alone, lost, abandoned). When des Grieux returns, she dies in his arms.

SUOR ANGELICA [swohr ahn-**geh**-lee-kah] (Sister Angelica)
Opera in 1 act
Libretto by Giovacchino Forzano
First performance: Metropolitan Opera, New York; December 14, 1918

This opera, the second part of *Il trittico* (The Triptych), is set in a convent near Siena in the seventeenth century. Sister Angelica, the daughter of a noble Florentine family, was forced to enter a convent after bearing a child out of wedlock seven years ago. Her aunt, the Princess, comes to ask her to sign away her inheritance. When Angelica asks for news about her child, she is told coldly that he died two years ago. She sings the heart-wrenching aria "Senza mamma" [**sehn**-zah **mahm**-mah] (Without a mother), then decides to commit suicide by drinking poison. In her dying moments she prays for forgiveness and sees a vision of the Virgin Mary bringing her child to her.

TOSCA [**taw**-skah]
Opera in 3 acts
Libretto by Giuseppi Giacosa and Luigi Illica, after the play by Sardou
First performance: Teatro Costanzi, Rome; January 14, 1900

This popular melodrama is set in Rome, June 1800. The painter Mario Cavaradossi is in love with Floria Tosca, a famous singer. While working on a mural in the church of Sant'Andrea della Valle, he sings the aria "Recondita armonia" [ray-**kohn**-dee-tahr-moh-**nee**-ah] (Secret harmonies), comparing the portrait of Mary Magdalene he is painting to the dark-eyed Tosca. Tosca soon arrives at the church, and they sing a duet, in which Tosca tells of "that sweet nest in which we love-birds hide" ("Non la sospiri" [nohn lah soh-**spee**-ree]). When Angelotti, an escaped political prisoner, appears at the church, Cavaradossi offers to help him by hiding him at his house. Angelotti was imprisoned by Scarpia, the sadistic and hypocritical chief of police, for being active in the uprising to make Rome a republic. Scarpia, who is also in love with Tosca, has Cavaradossi arrested, interrogated, and finally tortured in order to learn where Angelotti is hiding. Tosca, who can hear her lover's tortured screams, pleads in vain with Scarpia to show mercy to Cavaradossi. Finally, to stop the torture, Tosca discloses Angelotti's hiding place. Scarpia signs the warrant for Cavaradossi's execution, but tells Tosca that if she will give herself to him, he will spare her lover's life. In a moment of despair she sings "Vissi d'arte" [**vee**-see **dahr**-tay] (I lived for art), a passionate outpouring of grief. When she agrees to Scarpia's bargain, he says a mock execution must be carried out, after which Tosca and Cavaradossi are free to make a getaway. As he turns to embrace her, Tosca stabs Scarpia with a knife from his supper table, killing him. Meanwhile, Cavaradossi is imprisoned in the Castel Sant'Angelo, awaiting death at dawn. He sings "E lucevan le stelle" [ay loo-**chay**-vahn lay **stehl**-lay] (And the stars were shining), a poignant aria in which he remembers Tosca and their love. Tosca arrives and tells him of Scarpia's death and the plan for the fake execution. When Cavaradossi fails to get up after the firing squad has left (Tosca believes the bullets are blanks), Tosca suddenly realizes her lover is dead; Scarpia has tricked her. Scarpia has been found murdered, and as the soldiers come for her, Tosca runs to the edge of the battlements and jumps off, killing herself.

TURANDOT [too-rahn-doht]

Opera in 3 acts
Libretto by Giuseppe Adami and Renato Simoni, after Schiller's adaptation of the play *Turandotte* by Carlo Gozzi;
also possibly after *The Arabian Nights*
First performance: La Scala, Milan; April 25, 1926

The opera is set in Beijing in ancient times. The princess Turandot will marry the man who can solve three riddles; those who fail are summarily beheaded. Calaf, exiled prince of Tartary, is captured by her beauty and is willing to submit to the test, against the protests of his father, the exiled King Timus, and the faithful slave girl Liù, who is in love with him. Liù pleads with him to forgo his attempt, singing "Signore, ascolta" [seen-**yoh**-ray ah-**skol**-tah] (My lord, listen). Calaf wins the riddle contest, but Turandot still will not marry him. He, in turn, poses his own riddle for her: if she can tell him his name before daybreak, he will submit to execution. Turandot declares that no one shall sleep until the name of the prince is known, upon penalty of death. Calaf hears the injunction, but is unmoved. In "Nessun dorma" [**neh**-soon **dohr**-mah] (None shall sleep) he confidently states that he alone will unveil the secret, and when the sun is high in the heavens Turandot will indeed be his bride. Meanwhile, Timur and Liù are arrested and threatened with torture. Fearing for Timur's life, Liù says that she alone knows the name; she is tortured, but refuses to tell. When Turandot asks her what gives her such strength, she replies "Princess, it is love" ("Tanto amore segreto" [**tahn**-toh ah-**moh**-ray say-**gray**-toh]). In "Tu che di gel sei cinta" [too kay dee jehl say-ee **cheen**-tah] (You who are clothed in ice), the emotional climax of the opera, Liù addresses Turandot directly, then stabs herself with a soldier's dagger. Alone with the icy princess after Liù's suicide, Calaf tears off Turandot's veil, gives her a passionate kiss, and provides her with the opportunity to execute him by revealing his name. She calls for her court to be assembled and proclaims to all the stranger's name: Love.

LE VILLI [lay **veel**-lee] (The Willis)

Opera in 2 (originally 1) acts
Libretto by Ferdinand Fontata, after a popular folk legend, and perhaps after Adolphe Adam's ballet *Giselle*
First performance: Teatro dal Verme, Milan; May 31, 1884

Puccini's first opera, which he entered in a music publisher's contest for one-act works, is set in the Black Forest of Germany during olden (probably medieval) times. After Roberto falls prey to a seductress and abandons his betrothed, Anna, she dies of grief. Her spirit unites with the Willis, vengeful ghosts who prey on faithless lovers. In the end, Anna appears to Roberto and leads him a wild dance of death until he dies of exhaustion as the Willis cry "Hosanna!" The aria "Se come voi" [say **koh**-may voh-ee] (If I were like you) comes early in the opera, when Anna is very much in love with Roberto. She sings to a bouquet of forget-me-nots, symbols of fidelity, and places the flowers in Roberto's valise as a reminder of her love for him.

PIANO PIECES

Piccolo valzer ("Little waltz") was first published in a special edition of the magazine *Armi ed Arte* in September 1894. Several distinguished writers and composers had been invited to collaborate in honoring the presenting of the battle colors to the warship Umberto I. Puccini's inspiration for the piece is said to have come from the rocking of a boat on Lake Massaciuccoli, where he enjoyed fishing. Puccini later adapted it into one of his most famous opera arias, Musetta's "Quando men vo" in *La Bohème*.

Scossa elettrica ("Electric shock") was written in 1896 at the request of the Telegraphists' Committee to celebrate the centenary of the invention of the battery. This catchy little march was published by Ricordi, and was also scored for band performance.

Pezzo per pianoforte ("Piano piece") was composed at Puccini's home at Torre del Lago in 1916. It was published the same year in a booklet for the families of those killed in World War I. This somber and enigmatic composition, only sixteen measures long, is full of grief and sadness.

Che gelida manina

(How cold your little hand is)

LA BOHÈME

(The Bohemian Life)

Giacomo Puccini

Andantino affettuoso (♩ = 58)

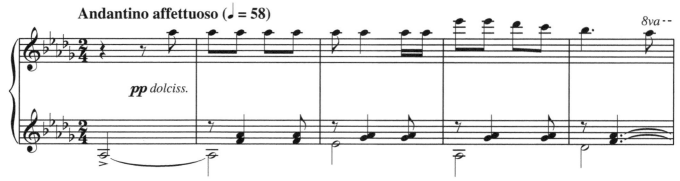

Andante sostenuto

Andante lento (♩ = 52)

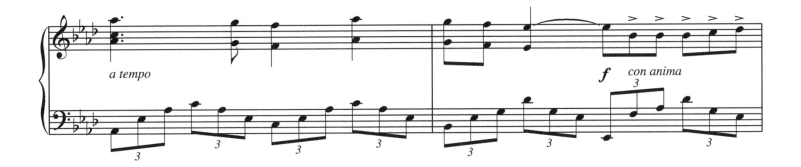

Mi chiamano Mimì

(I'm called Mimi)
LA BOHÈME
(The Bohemian Life)

Giacomo Puccini

Andante lento (♩ = 40)

Andante calmo (♩ = 54)

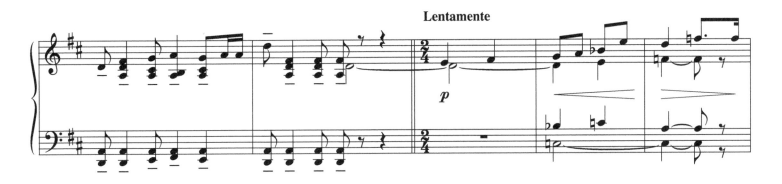

Lentamente

Allegro moderato (♩ = 144)

14

a piacere

a tempo

pp

Andante molto sostenuto

pp   cresc. poco a poco

ff   con grande espansione

pp   con espress. intensa

Andante calmo (♩ = 54)

O soave fanciulla

(O gentle woman)
LA BOHÈME
(The Bohemian Life)

Giacomo Puccini

Largo sostenuto (♩ = 58)

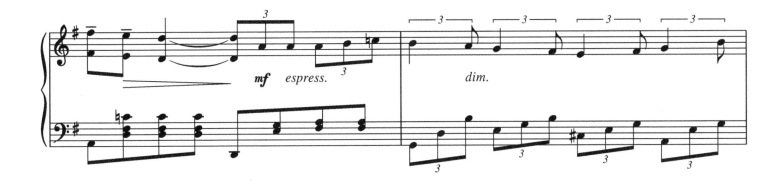

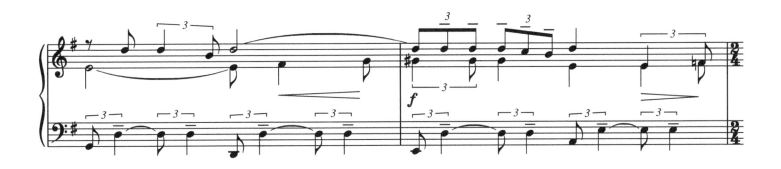

Quando men vo
(When I go out)
LA BOHÈME
(The Bohemian Life)

Giacomo Puccini

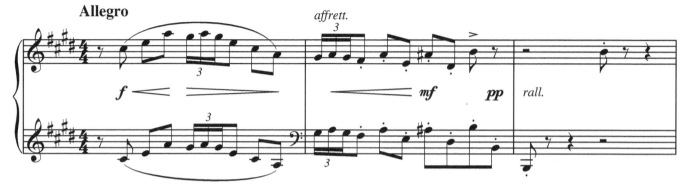

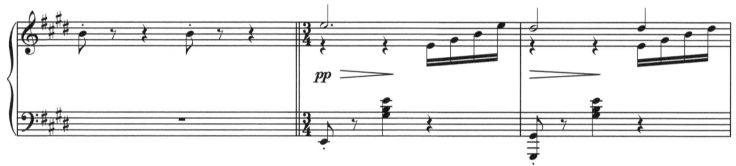

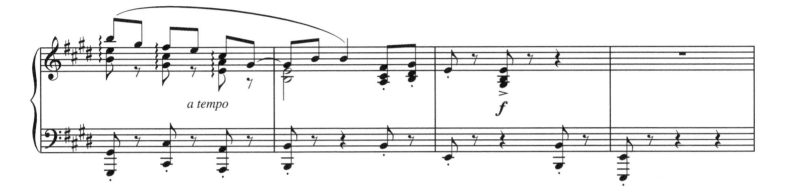

Act III Introduction
LA BOHÈME
(The Bohemian Life)

Giacomo Puccini

Andantino mosso (= 112)

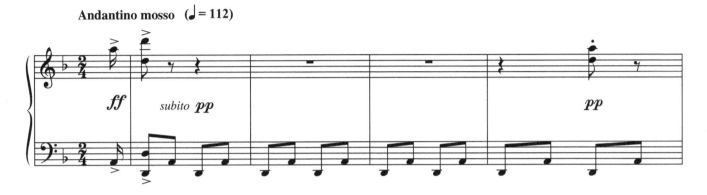

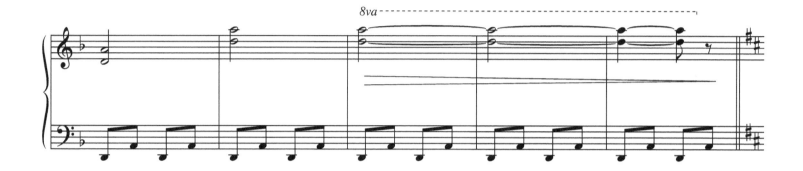

Donde lieta
(From the place she left)
LA BOHÈME
(The Bohemian Life)

Giacomo Puccini

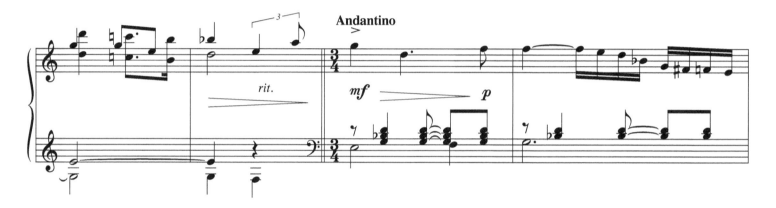

Andantino mosso (♩ = 84)

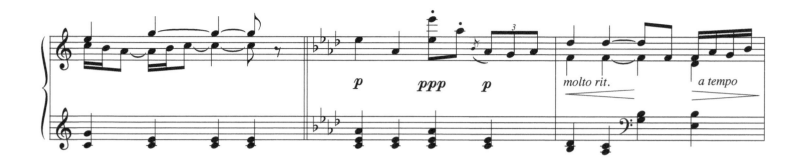

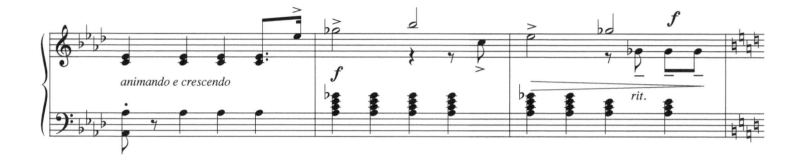

Mimi/Rodolfo Duet

(Act III)

LA BOHÈME

(The Bohemian Life)

Giacomo Puccini

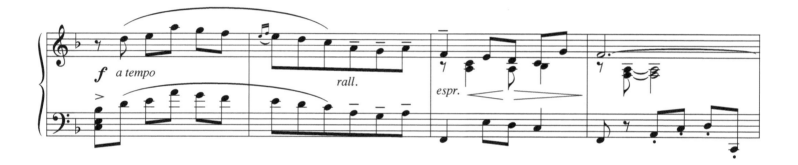

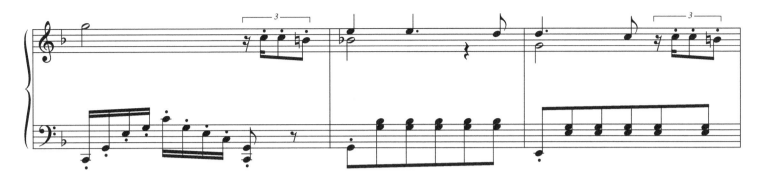

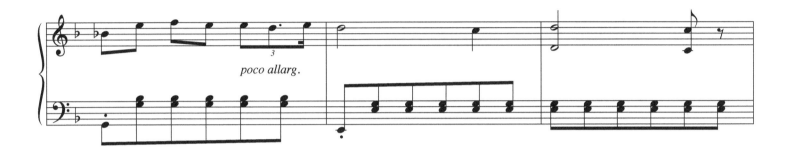

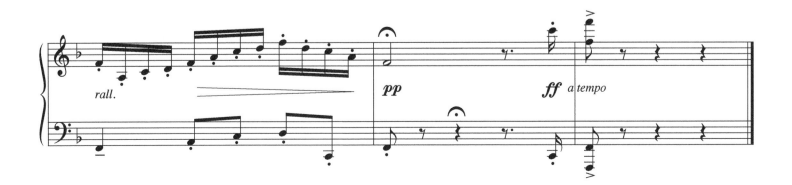

O Mimì, tu più non torni

(O Mimi, you do not return)

LA BOHÈME

(The Bohemian Life)

Giacomo Puccini

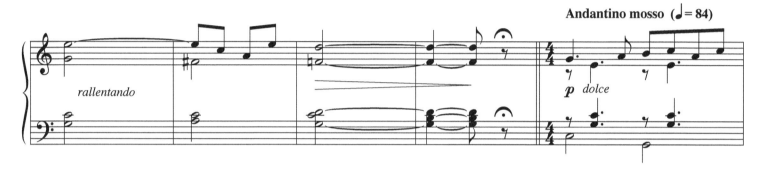

Vecchia zimarra
(Shabby old overcoat)
LA BOHÈME
(The Bohemian Life)

Giacomo Puccini

Allegretto moderato e triste (♩ = 63)

l.h. staccato

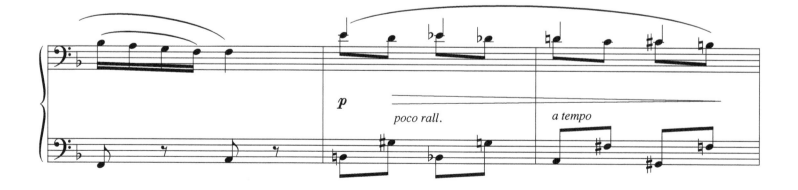

34

Sono andati

(Are they gone)
LA BOHÈME
(The Bohemian Life)

Giacomo Puccini

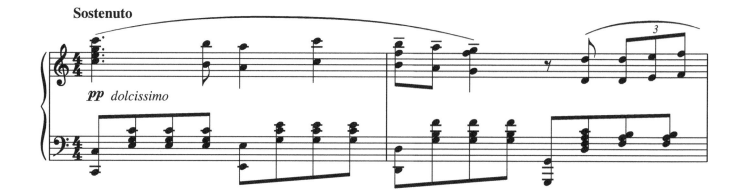

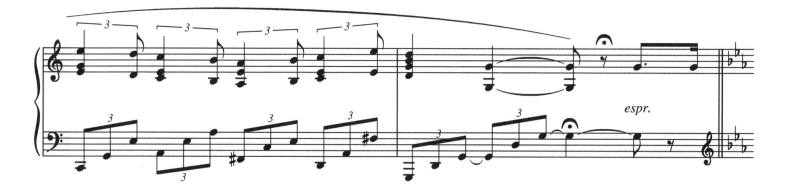

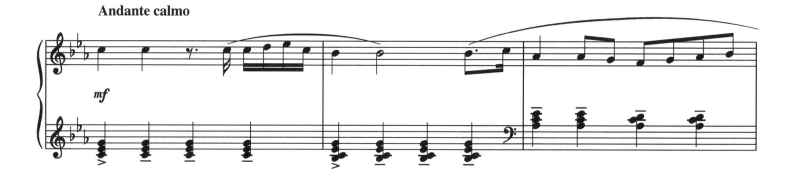

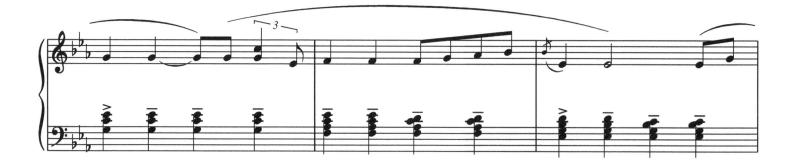

Minnie, dalla mia casa son partito

(Minnie, I left my home)
LA FANCIULLA DEL WEST
(The Girl of the Golden West)

Giacomo Puccini

Andante sostenuto (♩ = 60)

Ch'ella mi creda
(Let her believe)

LA FANCIULLA DEL WEST
(The Girl of the Golden West)

Giacomo Puccini

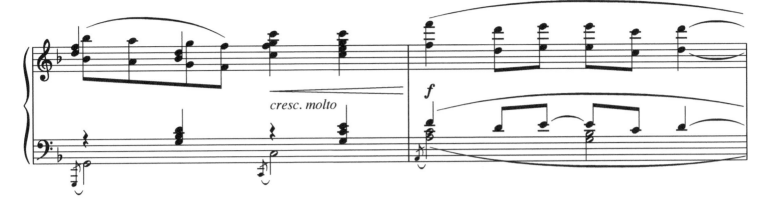

39

Rinuccio's Aria

(Firenze è come un albero fiorito)
GIANNI SCHICCHI

Giacomo Puccini

Andante sostenuto

Come il tempo primo
(Andante mosso)

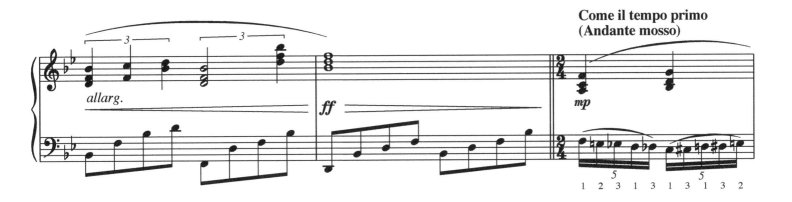

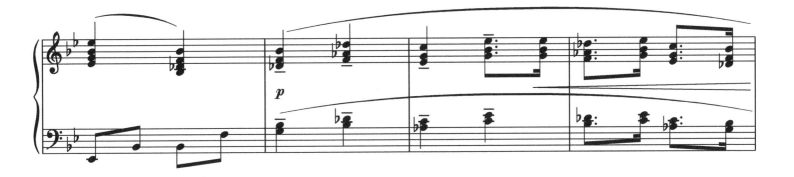

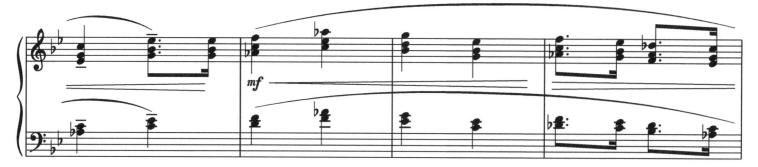

Un po' sostenuto

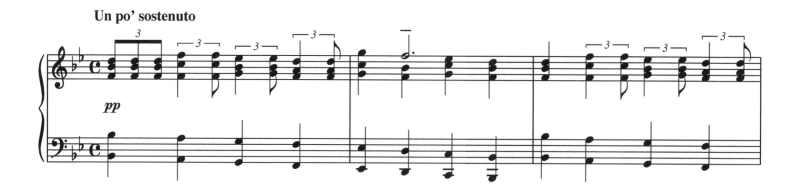

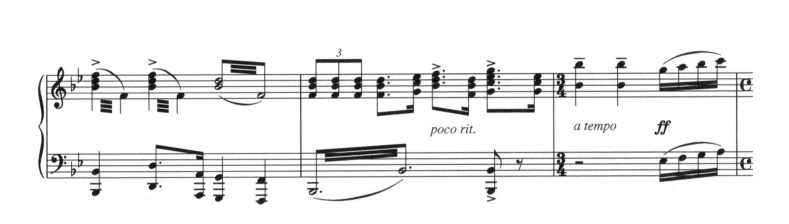

O mio babbino caro
(O my beloved daddy)
GIANNI SCHICCHI

Giacomo Puccini

Andante ingenuo (♪ = 120)

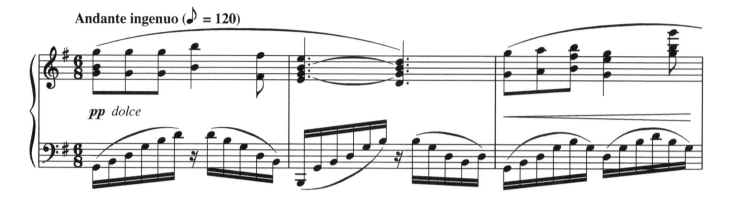

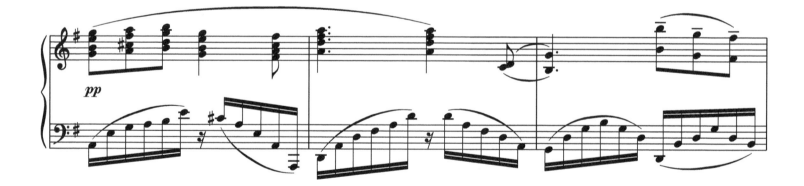

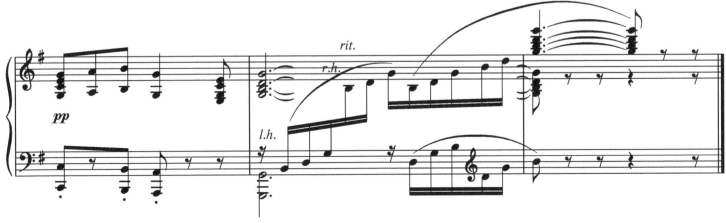

Love Duet
GIANNI SCHICCHI

Giacomo Puccini

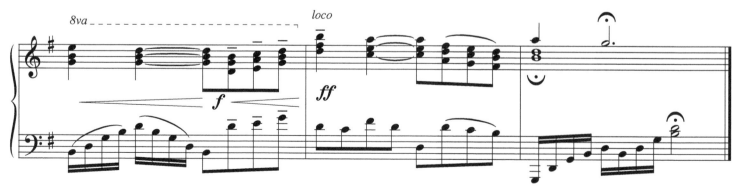

Amore o grillo
(Love or whim)
MADAMA BUTTERFLY

Giacomo Puccini

Allegro moderato (♩ = 104)

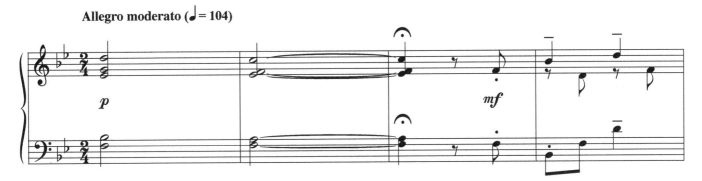

48

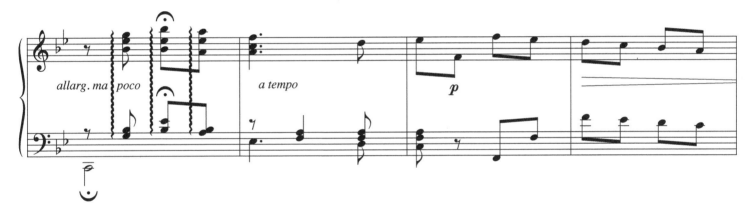

50

Un bel dì vedremo

(One fine day he will return)
MADAMA BUTTERFLY

Giacomo Puccini

Andante molto calmo (♩ = 42)

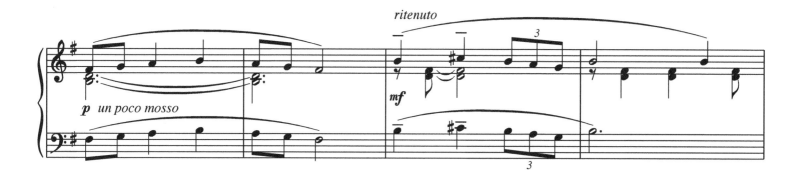

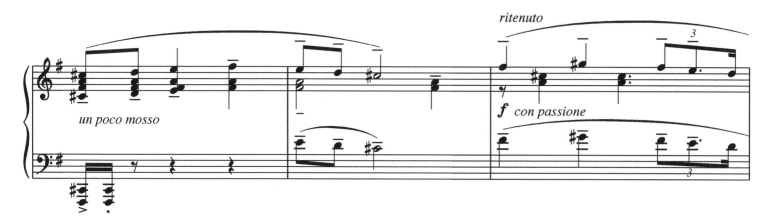

Copyright © 2002 by CASA RICORDI - BMG RICORDI S.p.A
Tutti i diritti riservati   All Rights Reserved

dolcemente   rall.

con semplicità

pp

pp   rit.   a tempo   p   animando un poco

p   rallentando un poco

Sostenendo molto
Lo stesso movimento

Lento

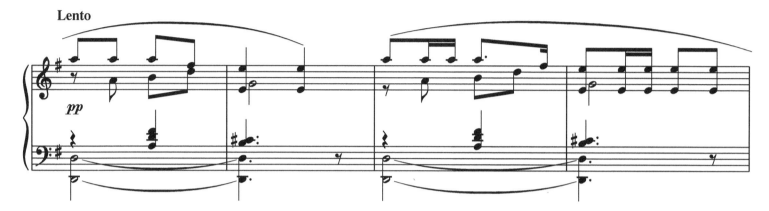

Andante come prima

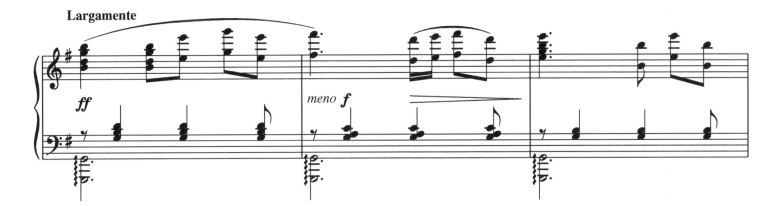

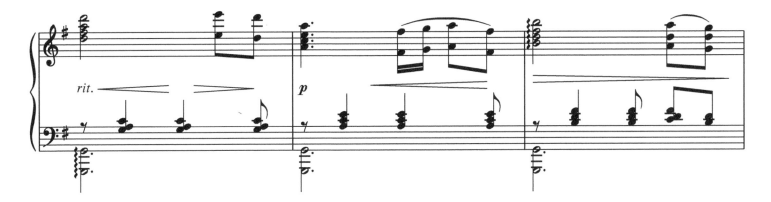

Addio, fiorito asil

(Farewell, happy home)

MADAMA BUTTERFLY

Giacomo Puccini

Andante sostenuto (♩ = 48)

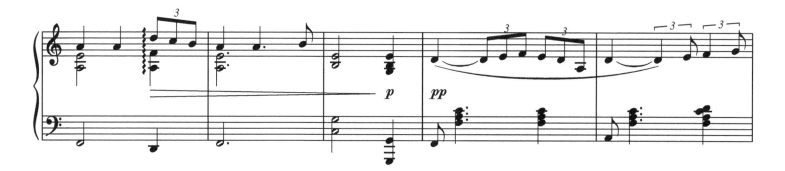

Entrance of Butterfly
MADAMA BUTTERFLY

Giacomo Puccini

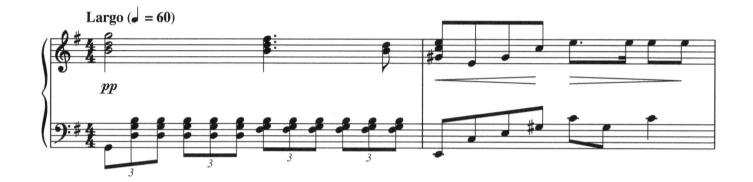

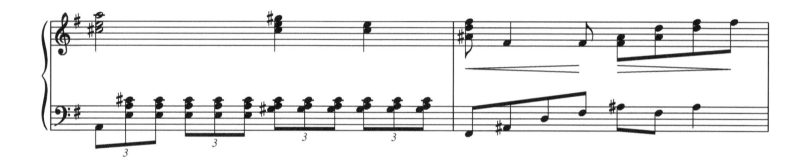

Sostenendo

Che tua madre

(That you mother)

MADAMA BUTTERFLY

Giacomo Puccini

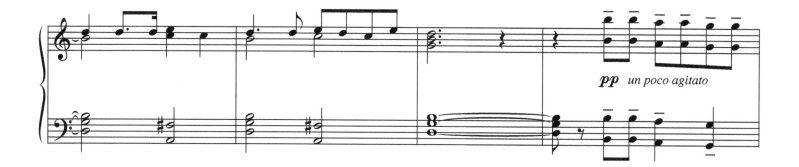

Flower Duet
MADAMA BUTTERFLY

Giacomo Puccini

Allegro moderato (♩. = 108)

63

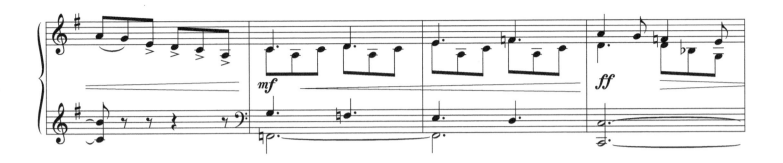

Un poco meno mosso

Intermezzo
MANON LESCAUT

Giacomo Puccini

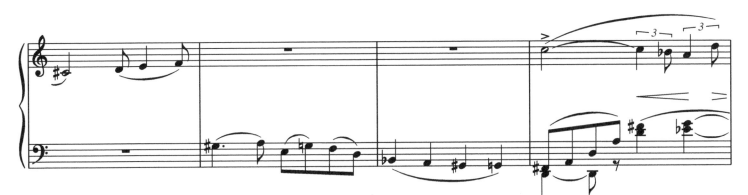

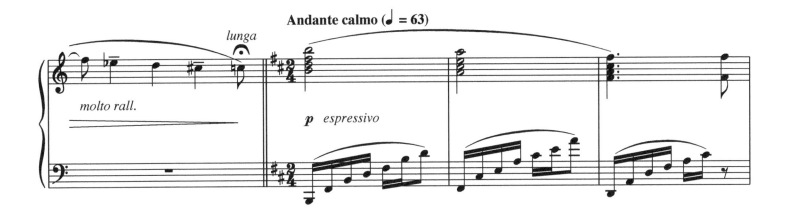

68

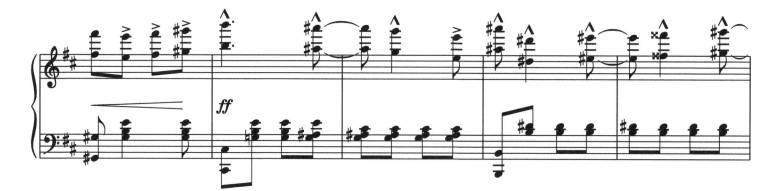

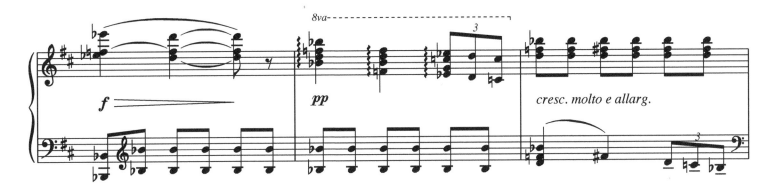

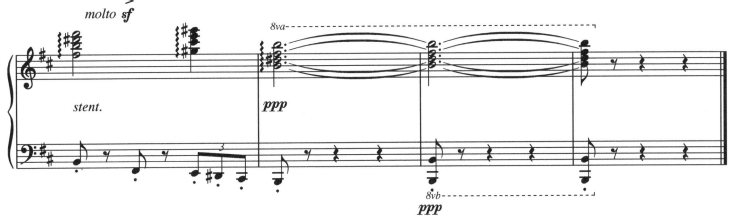

Donna non vidi mai
(I never saw such a beautiful woman)
MANON LESCAUT

Giacomo Puccini

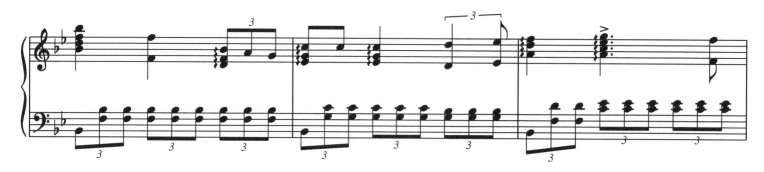

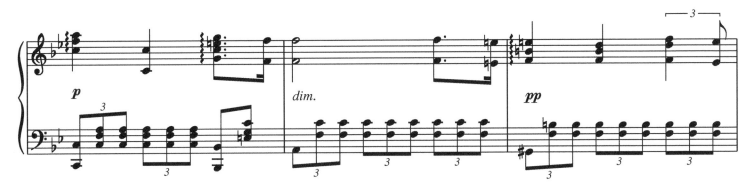

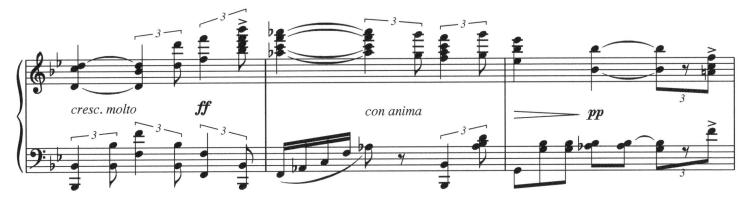

In quelle trine morbide

(In those soft curtains)

MANON LESCAUT

Giacomo Puccini

Moderato con moto ($\quad$ = 84)

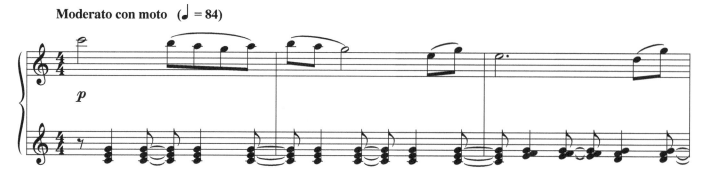

Sola, perduta, abbandonata
(Alone, lost, abandoned)
MANON LESCAUT

Giacomo Puccini

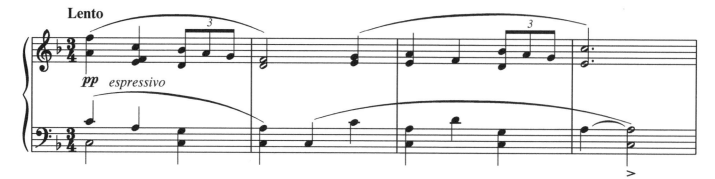

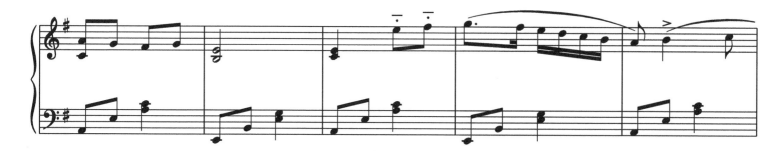

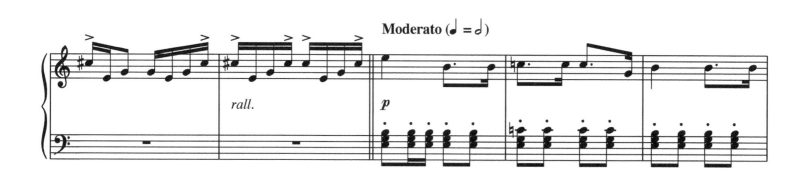

Largo molto sostenuto

Molto sostenuto

Senza mamma
(Without a mother)
SUOR ANGELICA
(Sister Angelica)

Giacomo Puccini

A tempo, ma ben sostenuto

Un poco meno, sostenendo

poco rit.   *a tempo*   *poco rit.*

Calmo

dim. e rall. molto   *ppp*   *pp*

rall.   *dim.*

Recondita armonia
(Secret harmonies)
TOSCA

Giacomo Puccini

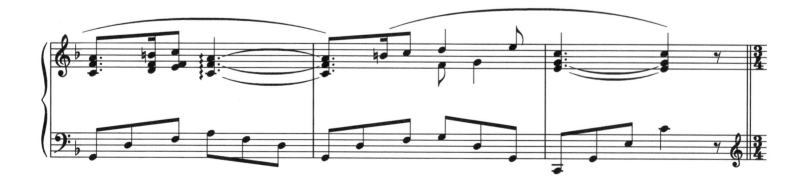

Lo stesso movimento

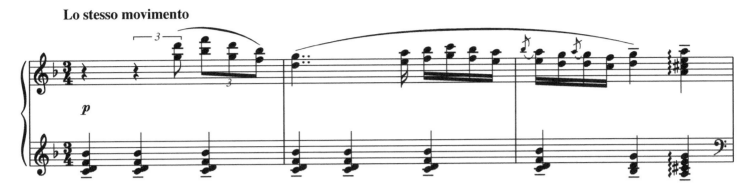

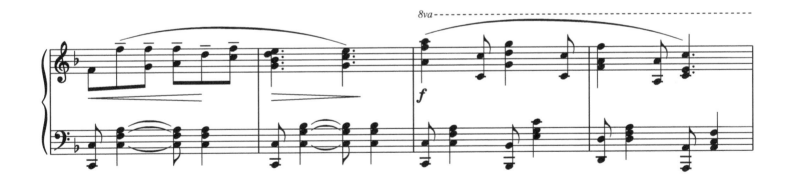

Non la sospiri

(Do you not yearn)

TOSCA

Giacomo Puccini

Allegro moderato (♩ = 116)

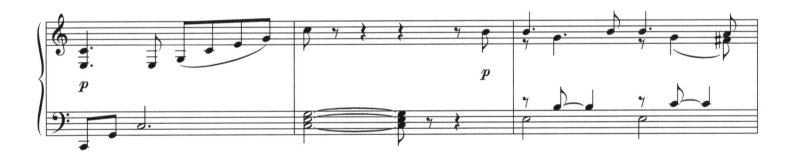

Vissi d'arte
(I lived for art)
TOSCA

Giacomo Puccini

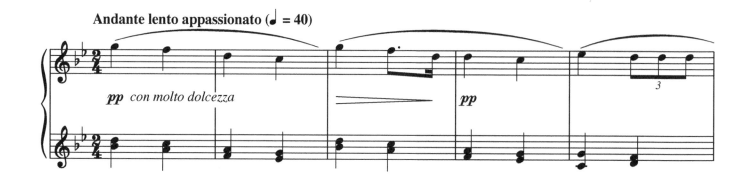

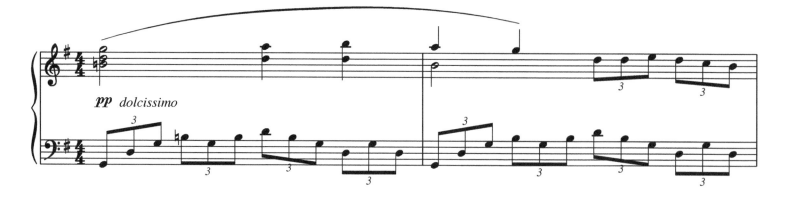

E lucevan le stelle

(And the stars were shining)

TOSCA

Giacomo Puccini

Lento, appassionato molto

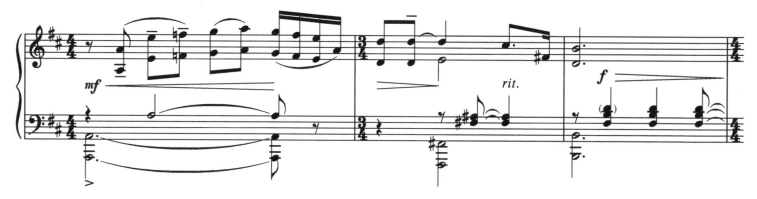

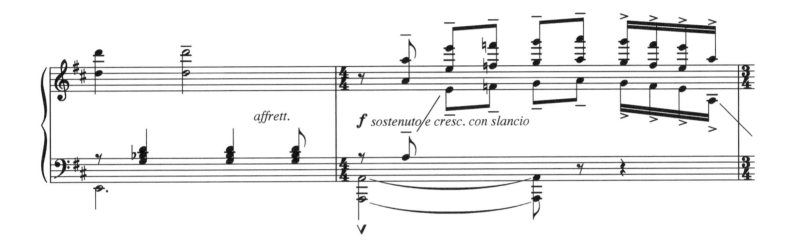

Nessun dorma
(None shall sleep)
TURANDOT

Giacomo Puccini

Andante sostenuto

Tanto amore segretto
(Great secret love)
TURANDOT

Giacomo Puccini

Lento (con grande tenerezza)

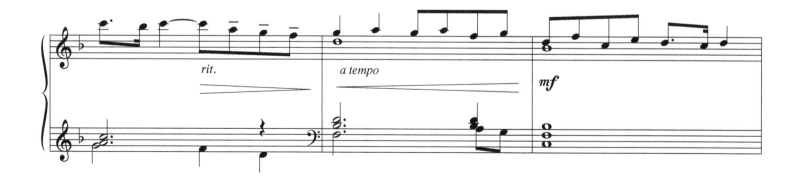

Tu che di gel sei cinta

(You who are clothed in ice)
TURANDOT

Giacomo Puccini

Signore, ascolta
(My lord, listen)
TURANDOT

Giacomo Puccini

Adagio (♩ = 50)

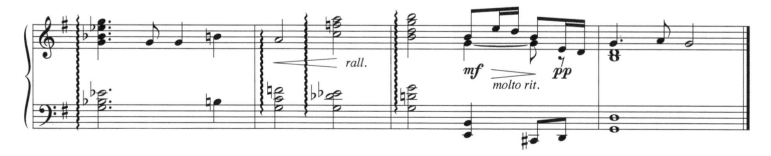

Se come voi

(If I were like you)
LE VILLI
(The Willis)

Giacomo Puccini

Andante lento

Andante espressivo

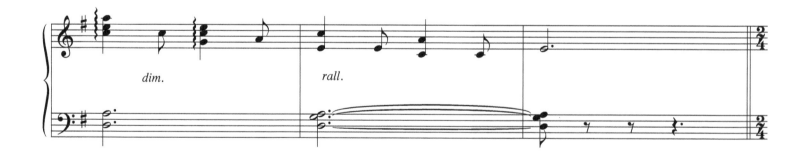

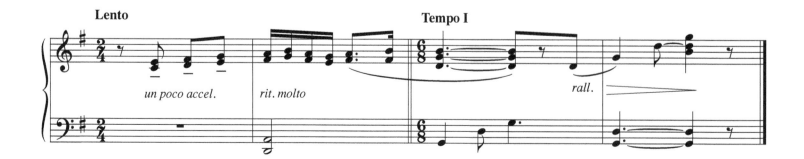

Piccolo valzer
(Little waltz)

Giacomo Puccini

Lento molto

pp con ondulazione

Scossa elettrica
(Electric shock)

Giacomo Puccini

Marcetta brillante

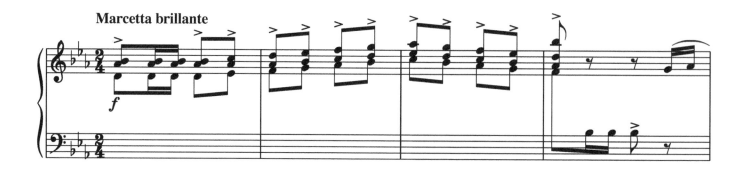

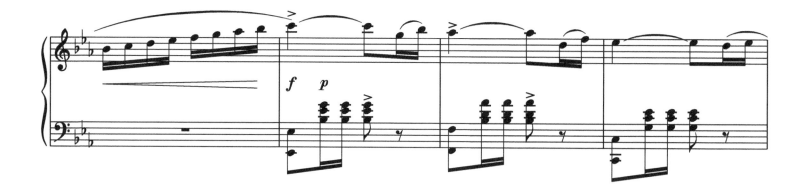

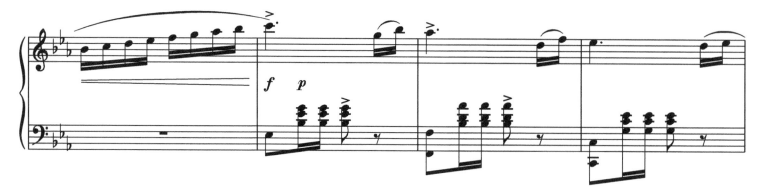

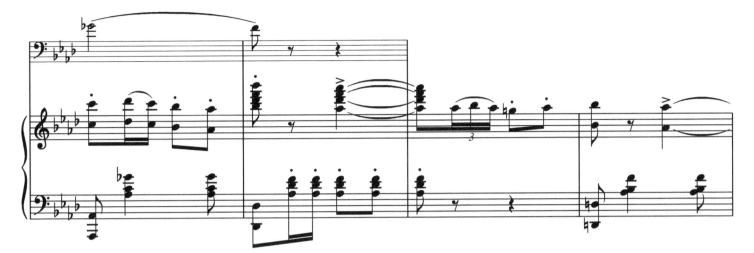

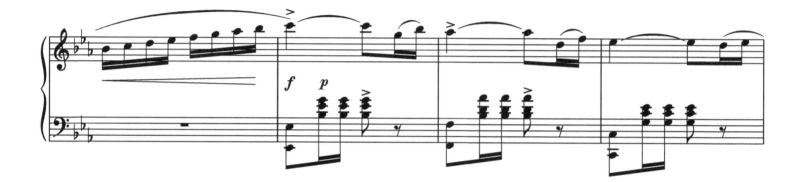

Pezzo per pianoforte
(Piano piece)

Giacomo Puccini

Calmo e molto lento

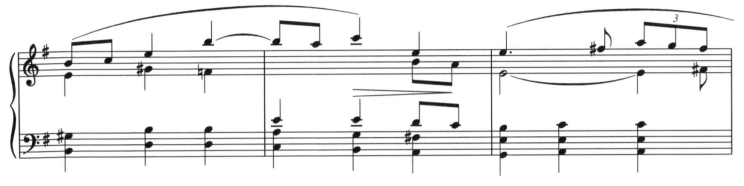

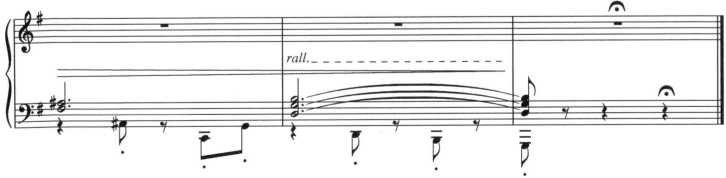